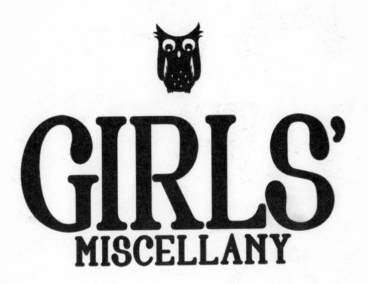

GIRLS'
MISCELLANY

Fascinating information
every girl should know

Written by Lottie Stride

Illustrated by Stefano Tambellini

Cover illustrations by Agnese Baruzzi

Edited by Sophie Schrey

Designed by Barbara Ward

Cover designed by Angie Allison

GIRLS'
MISCELLANY

Sandy Creek
NEW YORK

An Imprint of Sterling Publishing
387 Park Avenue South
New York, NY 10016

This 2013 edition published by Sandy Creek.
First published in Great Britain in 2012 by Buster Books,
an imprint of Michael O'Mara Books Limited.

The Sphinx on page 37 is by Simon Ecob
The image on page 48 is by Ann Kronheimer

ISBN 978-1-4351-5048-5

Manufactured by CPI Group (UK) Ltd, Croydon,
CR0 4YY, United Kingdom.

Lot #:
2 4 6 8 10 9 7 5 3 1
07/13

Contents

Which Is Worse?

None of the following things are enjoyable if they happen, but if you *had* to choose, which situation would be worse?

An ice-cream headache (also know as "brain freeze")

OR

Eating popcorn and chewing unexpectedly on a "kernel" (unpopped corn)

OR

stubbing your toe

OR

a top bunk and a low ceiling

OR

biting your tongue

OR

finding half a maggot in your apple.

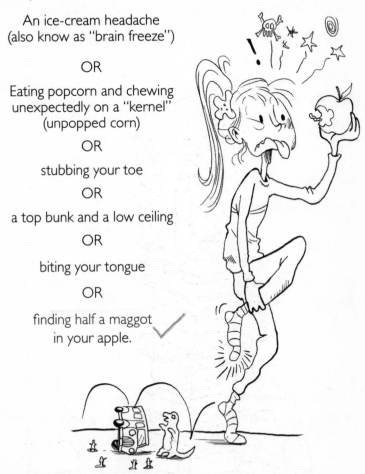

The *Titanic* set off on its fateful last voyage with 40,000 eggs, 36,000 oranges, and 16,000 lemons on board.

Weird Beauty Treatments

Forget a simple face wash and a good night's sleep, some people will go to much greater lengths in the name of beauty, even if the treatments do sound a bit weird and gross.

Beer bathing
A long soak in a bath of mineral water and foaming beer purifies your skin.

Carp pedicure
In a tank of water, tiny carp known as doctor fish nibble away dead skin on your feet.

Chocolate facial
A gooey cocoa-based mixture is spread on your face. This treatment has a double benefit because you can eat it afterward!

Seaweed wrap
A thick layer of seaweed is applied head to toe, covered in cling wrap, and then left for half an hour to help smooth skin.

Snail slime moisturizer
This is applied to help heal scars, blemishes, and acne.

Snake massage
Small snakes slither over skin to help soothe sore muscles. Not very relaxing if you have a fear of snakes!

Sense-Sational: Touch

The skin covering your whole body has tiny sensors, called receptors, that register touch. In 0.4 square inches of skin you have around 200 pain receptors, 15 pressure receptors, 6 receptors for cold and one receptor for warmth. Your tongue is very quick to feel pain, which is why biting it hurts so much, but strangely enough it's not as good at sensing hot or cold.

Top Ten Problems For Cave Girls

1. Forced to wear real fur.

2. They have to wait more than 30,000 years for electricity to be discovered – meaning no flat irons.

3. Unattractively large front teeth, a weak chin, and a significant amount of body hair.

4. Goat and mammoth are on the dinner menu far too often.

5. Forced to share a cave with their whole family and, quite possibly, whole tribe – urghh!

6. A high risk of breaking fingernails when using stone tools.

7. Hunting skills are top of the curriculum.

8. Faced with limited jewelry options.

9. Short and stocky build makes career as a supermodel out of the question.

10. No chocolate.

Roman Numerals

The Roman numeral system uses letters of the alphabet to represent numbers. Roman numerals are still used today, for example, to show dates on monuments and the hours on some watch or clock faces.

1 to 10	
1	I
2	II
3	III
4	IV
5	V
6	VI
7	VII
8	VIII
9	IX
10	X

11 to 20	
11	XI
12	XII
13	XIII
14	XIV
15	XV
16	XVI
17	XVII
18	XVIII
19	XIX
20	XX

11 TO 20 WORK IN THE SAME WAY AS NUMBERS 1 TO 10, BUT PUT X (FOR 10) IN FRONT.

FOLLOW THE SAME PATTERN FOR NUMBERS UP TO 100.

20 to 100

20	XX (XXI, XXII up to XXIX)
30	XXX (XXXI, XXXII up to XXXIX)
40	XL (XLI, XLII up to XLIX)
50	L (LI, LII up to LIX)
60	LX (LXI, LXII up to LXIX)
70	LXX (LXXI, LXXII up to LXXIX)
80	LXXX (LXXXI, LXXXII up to LXXXIX)
90	XC (XCI, XCII up to XCIX)

The hundreds

100	C
200	CC
300	CCC
400	CD or CCCC
500	D
600	DC
700	DCC
800	DCCC
900	CM
1,000	M

Examples of bigger numbers

107 = CVII

357 = CCCLVII

677 = DCLXXVII

1,827 = MDCCCXXVII

— 13 —

Number Facts – Roman Style

The number facts below are given in Roman numerals. Can you work out what the numbers are? The answers are at the bottom of the page.

I. Legend has it that Rome was founded by twin brothers named Romulus and Remus in DCCLIII BC.

II. Augustus became the first Emperor of Rome in XXVII BC.

III. The Romans first invaded Britain in LV BC.

IV. Soldiers marched up to XXXII km (XX miles) a day in armor.

V. The biggest Roman ships had more than CL oars.

VI. Many Roman girls married at the age of XIV.

VII. The last Romans left Britain in AD CDX.

OUCH! I'VE GOT A STITCH.

XVI

ANSWERS: 1. 753BC; 2. 27BC; 3. 55BC; 4. 32km (20 miles); 5 150 oars; 6. 14 years old; 7. AD410.

Really Useful Superpowers

Power to spin round in the bathroom and come out fully transformed for a party.

Power to erase the memories of all those around you who see when you trip over.

Power to shrink to ant-size when Mom comes looking for volunteers to do the dishes.

Power to open your mouth and produce the right answer to any question a teacher asks.

Power to turn vegetables into chocolate with one clap.

Power to send dazzling sparkles out of your eyes that make boys fall instantly in love with you.

Real Names Of Famous Singers

Katy Perry	Katheryn Elizabeth Hudson
Pink	Alecia Beth Moore
Rihanna	Robyn Rihanna Fenty
Madonna	Madonna Louise Ciccone
Lady Gaga	Stefani Joanne Angelina Germanotta.

Iceberg Sizes

Icebergs are the broken-off ends of "glaciers" (huge blocks of ice and snow that have built up over time) that float in the sea. Gradually they melt and disappear. Bergs vary greatly in size, and the tip of the iceberg – the bit that shows above the water – is only around one-eighth of its total size.

Smaller icebergs are known as growlers and bergy bits. They range from less than one meter (three feet) to four meters (13ft) above the water. These bergs can be very dangerous to ships because they are hard to spot. Very large icebergs are huge mountains of ice that reach up to 75m (246ft) above the water and can be up to 200m (656ft) long. Some icebergs are so huge that they travel more than 3,219km (2,000 miles) before they melt and disappear.

Things You Don't Want To Find In The Sea

A Kraken is a huge sea monster from northern European legend with far too many fins and horns. The monster dives underwater and makes vast whirlpools that suck ships down. The Kraken is able to devour entire fishing fleets – so girls on holiday are just a mere drop in the ocean. Or, to put it another way, a teeny tiny snack.

A Scolopendra comes from Greek myth. It is a vast creature and stupendously ugly, with a large snouty head, a body like a whale, and lots of long, bristly legs. If it swallows your fishing hook, it will throw up its own stomach, release the hook, and swallow its stomach again … nasty.

Mermaids

In 2012, the National Ocean Service, a part of the US government, made an official announcement declaring that there is no evidence of mermaids ever existing. They were forced to do it after they received enquiries from members of the public who had seen a TV show on mermaids and mistaken it for a science documentary. Sadly the program was a fishy work of fiction.

Which Way Are The Fish Swimming?

Women In A Man's World

Hua Mulan

The story of Mulan originates from an ancient Chinese poem. Mulan was the daughter of a 5th-century Chinese general called Hua Hu. He was old and ill when he was called to war, and Mulan was determined to protect him. So she disguised herself as a man and went to war in his place – pretending to be his son. She spent the next 12 years fighting battles for her country and became a legendary female warrior.

Anne Bonny

Irishwoman Anne Bonny traveled to the island of New Providence in the Bahamas, where she fell in love with a ruthless pirate called John "Calico Jack" Rackham. Anne's life as one of a feared band of notorious pirates of the Caribbean seas began. Disguised as a man, she fought fierce battles with cutlasses and guns, attacking ships along the coast of Jamaica and seizing their treasures. In 1720, their pirate ship was captured and all the men were hanged. Anne was put on trial, found guilty, and sentenced to death. However, her life was spared and it is thought that her father paid a ransom for her release.

Christian Welsh

When her husband, Richard Welsh, was forced to fight French forces in the Netherlands in the late 1600s, Christian Welsh (also known as Kit Cavanagh) disguised herself as a man and set out to find him. She joined the British Army, fighting in several major European battles, and after 13 years of searching the couple were reunited. It was only when Christian was wounded and had to have her wounds treated, that her true identity was discovered.

Calamity Jane

The Wild West, as western America was known, was a dangerous place to be in the late 1800s when Calamity Jane (real name Martha Jane Cannary) arrived. Bandits roamed the mountains and plains, robbing passing stagecoaches and wagon trains. Jane earned a living working in the saloons. She dressed like a man, drank, swore, and gambled. She was a fearless horsewoman and a crack shot with a rifle. Her legend grew fast and tales were told of how she rode the most dangerous routes delivering mail, risking ambush, and death. It is said her nickname came from her warning: "If you scorn Martha Jane Cannary, you court calamity." Or, in other words, "Mess with me and you're asking for disaster."

What Do Country Names Mean?

Argentina ············· land of silver   Netherlands ········· lower lands
Barbados ·········· bearded ones   Norway ·············· northern way
Costa Rica ················ rich coast   Portugal ············· beautiful port
Cyprus ······························ copper   Puerto Rico ·········· rich harbor
El Salvador ··············· the Savior   Sierra Leone ·· lion mountains
Estonia ····················· eastern way   Thailand ········· land of the free
Liechtenstein ········· light stone   Zimbabwe ··· houses of stone.

An Ocean Of Knowledge

The largest ocean, the Pacific, takes up a third of the Earth's surface. There are almost 30,000 islands in it, more than all the other oceans combined.

Sharks attack 50–75 people a year, killing 8–12, which is less than the number of people who are killed by bees, crocodiles, or elephants.

The lowest known point on the Earth's surface is called Challenger Deep, in the Mariana Trench in the western Pacific. It's 10,994m (36,069ft) deep. This means, if you put Mount Everest at the bottom of the trench, there would still be over 1.24 miles of ocean above it. In 2012, the filmmaker James Cameron became the first person to reach the bottom of Challenger Deep on a solo trip.

Blue whales are the biggest mammals that have ever lived on Earth, and the sea helps to support their huge weight. The blue whale's heart is the size of a small car.

A Selection Of Shells

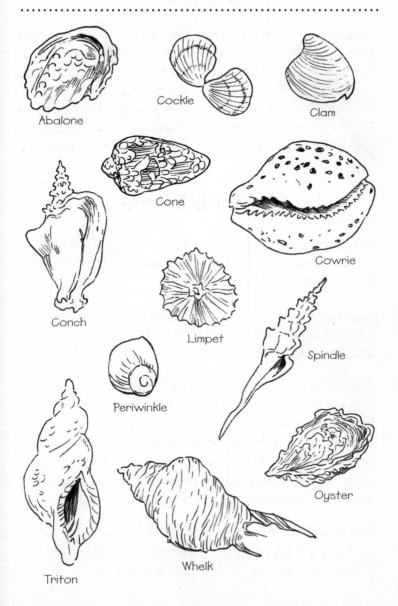

Abalone

Cockle

Clam

Cone

Cowrie

Conch

Limpet

Spindle

Periwinkle

Oyster

Triton

Whelk

Some Gruesome Girls From
Ancient Myths And Legends

Medusa

This gruesome girl was one of three sisters, known as Gorgons, from Greek mythology. Medusa was not a pretty sight. She had snakes for hair and one look from her turned people to stone. Luckily Medusa – unlike her ghastly sisters – was "mortal" (meaning she could die), and she had her head cut off by a Greek hero called Perseus.

Baba Yaga

This evil, witch-like woman comes from Slavic folklore. According to legend, Baba Yaga would kidnap small children and then eat them. She lived in a small hut supported by giant chicken legs.

Banshees

These wicked old women had glowing red eyes and lots of long wild hair. Banshees were best known for lurking around old Celtic families with "O" or "Mac" in their name, and wailing under the windows to warn the family that one of them was about to die. It was believed that whichever person was unlucky enough to hear their screams was likely to drop dead soon after.

Harpies

It could be said that the horrid harpies were members of the first ever girl gang. They were foul-smelling demon spirits of the wind, who roamed around in groups, had bird bodies, arms with talons for fingers, and hideous human faces. One touch from their talons turned things poisonous and rotten.

Sirens

These vicious spirits of the sea are also from Greek myth. They hung about on the rocks around the island of Sicily, off the coast of Italy, singing bewitching songs in beautiful voices. Passing sailors all fell in love with their singing and ended up crashing their boats against the rocks – by which point it was too late to realize they had been lured to certain death. Talk about being blinded by love!

Baby Baby

A "litter" is the name given to a group of baby animals that are born to one mother at the same time. The number of young in each litter varies between animals.

Rabbits

Average of 7 bunnies per litter.

Length of pregnancy: 30 days.

Elephants

1 calf or occasionally twins.

Length of pregnancy: 18–22 months.

Camels

1 calf per litter.

Length of pregnancy: 13 months.

Dogs (large)

Average of 8 puppies per litter.

Length of pregnancy: 63 days.

Dogs (small)

2–3 puppies per litter.

Length of pregnancy: 63 days.

Whale
1 calf or occasionally twins.

Length of pregnancy: 9–12 months.

Hamsters
Average of 5–10 pups per litter.

Length of pregnancy: 16 days.

Cats
Average of 4 kittens per litter.

Length of pregnancy: 63–65 days.

Horses
1 foal, occasionally twins or triplets.

Length of pregnancy: 11 months.

Mice
Baby mice are called pups, pinkies, or kittens. There are 6–11 per litter.

Length of pregnancy: 21 days.

Female seahorses leave pregnancy to the boys. They pop up to 300 eggs in the male seahorse's pouch, and he looks after them until they hatch, about four weeks later.

Key Moments In Toilet History

The royal wee

3000–1500BC: The royal folk in the Palace of Knossos, on the Greek island of Crete, are using toilets consisting of a seat and pan, with a system of drains and pipes to dispose of the royal poo.

Rest your legs (and arm)

Around 200BC: Some Chinese can relieve themselves in comfort. Their toilets are built of stone, with pipes for flushing running water, and arm rests. Relaxing!

Share the love

753BC–AD410: Ancient Romans make visits to the bathroom a group activity. They build marble benches with lines of holes above ditches with water running through them. In the absence of toilet paper, they share a wet sponge tied to the end of a stick.

A posh poo

Around 1400: The King of France has a padded seat in his palace, equipped with a 25m (82ft) shaft that descends into the depths of the palace to take the royal waste away.

Meanwhile . . . poor people's poo

Ordinary citizens use chamber pots, that they empty out of windows and on to the street – or on to unlucky passers-by. People often shout "gardez l'eau" (pronounced *gar-day low*), a French term meaning "watch out for the water."

Don't forget to flush

By the late 1500s: John Harrington, the godson of Queen Elizabeth I of England, develops a flushing toilet. Elizabeth installs John's toilets in all her palaces, but no one else really takes up the idea.

No need to hold your nose

Late 1700s: Alexander Cummings improves Harrington's design, creating an S-curved water pipe underneath the basin of the toilet to trap foul smells. In the 1880s, the flushing toilet goes into production thanks to Thomas Crapper.

Heavy, Heavier, Heaviest

A list of the weightiest human organs, starting with the heaviest.

Kidneys • Heart • Lungs • Brain • Liver • Skin

What Is Made Where?

Sweat is made in glands in your skin.

Blood is made in your bone marrow.

Urine is made in your kidneys.

Blood Types

Did you know that not all blood is the same? People can have different blood types (or groups). There are four main blood types: A, B, AB and O. Sometimes people need to be given blood that has been donated by other people – known as a transfusion. Your blood group affects who you can give blood to, and who you can receive blood from.

Blood type	Can give to	Can receive from
A	A and AB	A and O
B	B and AB	B and O
AB	AB	A, B, AB, and O
O	A, B, AB, and O	O

Interesting "Ologists"

A word that ends in "ology" relates to the study of something. An "ologist" is a person who is a specialist in that thing. Here are some examples.

Archaeologist
Finds out about human history and how people lived by studying physical remains.

Palaeontologist
Studies fossils, which are parts of plants, animals, and people that over thousands or millions of years have turned to stone.

Psychologist
Studies the human mind, how it works, and how we behave.

Zoologist
Studies animals, and searches out new species.

Trichologist
Studies hair and finds out about its structure and diseases.

Seismologist
Studies earthquakes.

Geologist
Studies the structure of the Earth, especially its rocks.

Mary, Mary

Mary, Queen of Scots became Queen of Scotland in 1542, when she was still a baby. As an adult she was unpopular and she fled to England to escape her enemies. Mary had hoped that Elizabeth, her cousin and the Queen of England, would help her. Instead Elizabeth had her imprisoned, then beheaded. So much for a warm welcome!

Marie Curie was born in Poland and was one of the most famous scientists of her time. Her discoveries were crucial in the development of X-rays in surgery. She was awarded two Nobel Prizes, one with her husband, Pierre, for Physics in 1903, and another for Chemistry in 1911.

Mary Phelps Jacob wanted to wear a dress to a party in New York in 1913, but her corset was too big to fit underneath. Instead, she wore two silk handkerchiefs tied together with ribbon. The idea caught on, and she set up a company to sell her invention. She called it a "brassiere." Today we know it as a bra.

Mary Anderson developed the first working design for a windscreen wiper, after watching people stuggle to clear their windscreens during a snowstorm on a journey to New York in 1903. By 1913, many American cars had Mary's windscreen wipers.

Marie Tussaud learnt the art of wax sculpting as a child in Paris. After the French Revolution in 1792, when the French monarchy was overthrown, Marie was given the gruesome task of making wax death-masks of the victims who had been beheaded on the guillotine. In 1835, she founded Madame Tussauds wax museum in London.

The World's Longest

Coastline: Canada, 243,792km (151,480 miles)

Snake: Royal python, 10m (32ft)

River: Nile, 6,695km (4,160 miles)

GREAT VIEW FROM UP HERE!

132cm (51.9in)

Catwalk: 2,292km (7,519ft), erected in Belgium, 8th October 2011

Cave: Mammoth Cave System, Kentucky, USA. So far over 627.6km (390 miles) have been explored.

Human bone: Femur (thigh bone), average adult male 50cm (19.7in)

Road tunnel: Laerdal, Norway, 24,510m (80,413ft)

Underground rail network: Shanghai, 420km (261 miles)

Earthworm: found in South Africa, 6.7m (22ft) fully extended

Hair on a woman: Xie Qiuping (China), 5.627m (18ft 5.5in)

Legs on a woman: Svetlana Pankratova (Russia), 132cm (51.9in).

A

36

D F

24

H Z P

18

T X U D

12

Z A D N H

9

P N T U H X

6

U A Z N F D T

5

N P H T A F X U

4

X D F H P T Z A N

3

Eye Test

Think you've got eyes like a hawk? Use this chart to to find out.

Stand 2.25 meters (7 feet 5.5 inches) from the page. If you can read down to the seventh line, your vision is normal. If you can read all the way to the bottom line, your vision is better than average. (If you can't read the top line, you should probably make an appointment with an optician.) The numbers on the chart indicate the height of the letters in millimeters.

Eye-Opening Facts

It's time to set your sights on the animal kingdom, with some amazing facts about animal eyes.

- A golden eagle has super-strength sight and can see a rabbit on the ground up to 3.2km (2 miles) away. Run, rabbit, run!

- Sleep is a risky business for dolphins because they need to swim to the surface for air regularly. Rather than completely passing out, like other mammals, they sleep with one eye open. This allows them to rest one half of their brain while the other half stays alert so they can swim to the surface and also be aware of potential predators.

- There's no need to wear goggles if you're a penguin – they have see-through eyelids so they can swim with their eyes shut and still see where they are going.

- Don't get on the wrong side of a horned lizard. If they feel threatened, these North American reptiles shoot blood from their eye-sockets up to a distance of 1.2m (4ft).

GULP!

Which Is Fastest?

Some animals can reach super-speeds, while others can't quite catch up. Come on, zebra, you can do it!

Ostrich
45m/h (70km/h)

Zebra
35m/h (55km/h)

Gazelle
47m/h (76km/h)

What Are The Odds?

What are the chances of cracking open an egg and finding it contains a double yolk? Some crazy calculators will try to work out the odds for anything. Here are some of their results (but don't take them too seriously).

- 1 in 1,000 chance of finding a double-yolked egg
- 1 in 10,000 chance of finding a four leaf clover
- 1 in 365 chance of sharing the same birthday as your friend
- About a 1 in 3,000,000 chance of being struck by lightning. Coincidentally, these are the same chances as meeting an alien, which might be more fun.

Lion
50m/h (80km/h)

Cheetah
70m/h (113km/h)

Types Of Lightning

Bead • Chain • Cloud-to-ground • Forked • Ribbon
• Rocket • Sheet • Streak • Staccato

1961

Was the last year to read the same the right way up and
upside down. Turn the book upside down to see!

Inventions

You will probably encounter some of these inventions on a daily basis – but when were they first created?

What	When	What	When
Sewing machine	1830	Ballpoint pen	1938
Safety pin	1849	Microwave oven	1946
Escalator	1900	CD	1982
Electric light bulb	1878	World Wide Web (Internet)	1990
Electric toaster	1909		
Television	1925	DVD	1995

Little Inventions That Are A Big Help

Hooray for these small yet ingenious inventions. Where would you be without them?

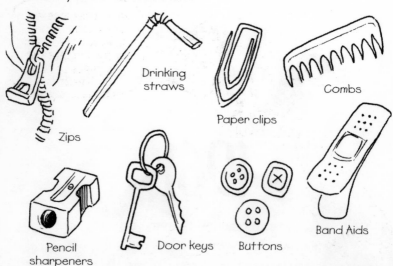

Zips

Drinking straws

Paper clips

Combs

Pencil sharpeners

Door keys

Buttons

Band Aids

The Sphinx

The Sphinx was a monster from Greek myth. She had the head of a beautiful young woman, the body and legs of a lion, the wings of an eagle, and the tail of a serpent. The Sphinx sat on a rock outside the Greek city of Thebes and demanded that travelers answer her riddle before she'd let them pass. If they couldn't answer – and they never could – she ripped them apart and ate them.

Luckily for the people of Thebes, a brainy hero called Oedipus came along and got the answer to her riddle right. The Sphinx was so shocked that she fell off her rock, tumbled over a very high, very steep cliff, and broke her neck.

Can you solve the Sphinx's riddle? Turn to page 39 for the answer.

WHAT CREATURE HAS FOUR LEGS IN THE MORNING, TWO LEGS IN THE AFTERNOON, AND THREE LEGS IN THE EVENING?

Popular City Attractions

If you are a city girl there are so many beautiful and exciting places to explore around the world. Here is a whirlwind tour of a handful of cities and the attractions you should be sure not to miss on your travels.

	Paris (France)	Tokyo (Japan)	Sydney (Australia)
Building	Eiffel Tower	Meiji Shrine	Opera House
Museum	Louvre Museum	Tokyo National Museum	The Australian Museum
River	Seine	Sumida	Hawkesbury
Park	Bois de Boulogne	Yoyogi Park	Royal National Park

Answer to the Sphinx's riddle: Man.
A baby crawls on all fours, he stands on two feet as a man, and uses a stick to help him walk when he's old. The stages of the day represent the different stages in human life. The morning is the first stage, when you are a baby, and the evening is the end of the day, when you are old.

London (England)	Moscow (Russia)	New York (USA)
Houses of Parliament	Kremlin	Empire State Building
British Museum	Tretyakov Gallery	Metropolitan Musem of Art
Thames	Moskva	Hudson
Regent's Park	Gorky Park	Central Park

Types Of Currency

Every globetrotting girl needs to know which "currency" (the system of money that is used in a particular country) to put in her purse.

Australia	Australian dollar (100 cents)
Bangladesh	taka (100 poisha)
Brazil	real (100 centavos)
China	yuan (10 jiao or 100 fen)
Croatia	kuna (100 lipa)
France	euro (100 cents)
Gambia	dalasi (100 butut)
India	rupee (100 paisa)
Japan	yen (100 sen)
Maldives	rufiyaa (100 laaris)
Mexico	peso (100 centavos)
Papua New Guinea	kina (100 toea)
Poland	zloty (100 groszy)
Russia	rouble (100 copecks)
Sweden	krona (100 öre)
Turkey	lira (100 kurus)
UK	pound (100 pence)
USA	dollar (100 cents).

Types Of Nut

Almond • Brazil nut • Cashew • Coconut • Chestnut • Hazelnut • Macadamia • Pecan • Pistachio • Walnut

Size It Up

Here's a handy guide to the different measurements that are used for women's clothes and shoes. Sizes vary between manufacturers, so use this for guidance only, and try before you buy to make sure you always get the perfect fit.

Dress sizes

UK	6	8	10	12	14	16	18	20
US	4	6	8	10	12	14	16	18
European	34	36	38	40	42	44	46	48

Shoe sizes

UK	2	3	4	5	6	7	8	9
US	4	5	6	7	8	9	10	11
European	35	35½	37	38	39½	41	42	43

Ten Famous Shopping Streets

- Calle Serrano, Madrid, Spain
- Champs-Elysées, Paris, France
- Oxford Street, London, UK
- Rodeo Drive, Los Angeles, USA
- Wangfujing Street, Beijing, China
- Kurfürstendamm, Berlin, Germany
- Pitt Street Mall, Sydney, Australia
- Tverskaya Ulitsa, Moscow, Russia
- Via dei Condotti, Rome, Italy
- Ginza district, Tokyo, Japan.

What To Do In A Thunderstorm

Thunder and lightning can be exciting, but frightening, too. Here are some tips on how to stay safe if you are caught in a thunderstorm – indoors or out.

Indoors: You should avoid touching taps and sinks because metal pipes conduct electricity. Don't use phones with wire leads except in an emergency.

Outdoors: The key is to stay low to the ground. Keep away from the tops of hills and find a low-lying open place to stay until the storm passes. Steer clear of water – it conducts electricity. Avoid tall trees, poles, and metal objects and don't use an umbrella. Try to touch as little ground as possible and don't lie down. If your skin tingles or hair stands on end, it means lightning is about to strike. Crouch down immediately, with your hands on your knees and your head tucked in.

Discovery Of Coffee

Legend has it that around 850, an Ethiopian goatherder became puzzled by the bizarre behavior of his goats, who appeared to be very frisky and alert. He decided to sample berries from the same bush his herd had been feeding from. To his amazement, he too began to feel pretty perky and he proclaimed his discovery to the world – coffee!

The bush in question was the tropical evergreen coffee plant. Today it is grown for its seeds or beans, which are roasted and ground before being used to brew coffee.

Types Of Coffee

Here is a handy guide to some different kinds of coffee, so the next time you are in a café you'll know exactly what to order.

Strong shot of black coffee

Espresso

Hot water

Espresso shot

Americano

Steamed milk

Espresso

Macchiato

Milk foam

Steamed milk

Espresso

Latte

Chocolate shavings (optional)

Foaming steamed milk

Espresso

Cappuccino

Dollop of whipped cream

Steamed milk

Chocolate syrup

Espresso

Mocha

The waltz is a graceful, elegant dance. The steps below will teach you how to do the "box step," the most common step used in the waltz. Practie with a friend, taking it in turns to be the leader (the steps below are given for the leader). The other person mirrors the leader's movements all the way through.

Facing each other, put your right hand on your partner's waist, slightly round the back. Lift your left arm out to the side, palm raised. Your partner puts her left hand on your right shoulder, and her right hand in your left hand.

The steps for the leader

Beat one: Step forward on your left foot. (Your partner mirrors all your movements so, in this case, steps back with her right foot).

Beat two: Step forward and right with your right foot, tracing an upside-down L above the ground as you go.

Keep your left foot still and shift your weight to the right foot.

Beat three: Slide your left foot over to your right and put your feet together.

Beat four: Step back with your right foot.

Beat five: Step back and left with your left foot, again tracing the L shape above the ground as you go. Keep your right foot still and shift your weight to your left foot.

Last beat: Slide your right foot over to your left and put your feet together.

Now start again with your left foot, and repeat all six steps.

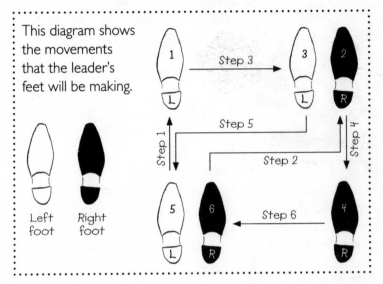

This diagram shows the movements that the leader's feet will be making.

Left foot   Right foot

Step 3

Step 1   Step 5   Step 4

Step 2

Step 6

Tips

• Count "one – two – three, one – two – three" as you do the steps, putting emphasis on the "one" each time.

• The aim of the waltz is to work your way around the ballroom floor. As you waltz, keep turning your partner gradually more to the left, by slightly changing where you put your feet. Try to achieve a gliding, graceful style.

The waltz started its life in the 18th century, probably evolving from German and Austrian folk dances.

Wives Of Henry VIII

Henry VIII was King of England from 1509 to 1547. He ate a lot, drank a lot, and grew extremely fat during his 38-year reign. But he was probably most famous for having six wives.

1. Catherine of Aragon
(married 1509/divorced 1533)

All of Catherine's children died except one, a girl called Mary. Daughters were no good to Henry, who wanted a son and heir. He was also already secretly in love with Wife 2. He divorced Catherine.

2. Anne Boleyn
(married 1533/beheaded 1536)

Anne also failed to provide a male heir and had a baby girl. So Henry got fed up with Anne, too, and had her beheaded. Some say her ghost still wanders around the Tower of London with its head tucked under one arm.

3. Jane Seymour
(married 1536/died 1537)

Henry married Jane less than two weeks after Anne's beheading. It is said Jane was his favorite wife but, alas, she died 12 days after giving birth to the long-awaited son and heir, Edward.

4. Anne of Cleves
(married 1540/divorced 1540)

Marriage number four was not a success. Henry was shown a painting of a pretty German girl and told it was a good idea to marry her. It wasn't. Henry took one look at Anne, decided she wasn't half as pretty as the painting, and divorced her within six months.

5. Catherine Howard
(married 1540/beheaded 1542)

Catherine married Henry soon after his divorce but only managed two years before he discovered she had a secret boyfriend, and – you guessed it – had her beheaded.

6. Catherine Parr
(married 1543/survived)

She outlived Henry. Well done, Catherine!

This catchy little rhyme is a cool way to remember the fate of each wife:

Divorced, beheaded, died,
Divorced, beheaded, survived.

How Many?

3	Finger holes in a bowling ball
5	Eyes on a bee
6	Strings on a guitar
7	Players in a water polo team
8	Notes in an octave
10	Legs on a shrimp
11	Players in a hockey team
26	Bones in your foot
52	Playing cards in a deck
78	Calories in an average large-sized egg
142	Staircases in Hogwarts School of Witchcraft and Wizardry
366	Days in a leap year
1,440	Minutes in a day
31,536,000	Seconds in one non-leap year.

A Hoppy Wedding

Green was the color scheme of choice at this wedding, when two frogs were married in front of 2,000 guests at a ceremony in northwest India. Sadly, neither of the frogs turned into a prince after being kissed, although the couple were said to be very happy and they spent their honeymoon downstream. An ancient tradition said that the marriage would help to end water shortages in the region.

Vampires – The Facts

- Leave their graves at night to attack the living
- Have long pointed front teeth
- Can fly like bats
- Cast no shadow

- Have no reflection in mirrors
- Use teeth to puncture skin and suck out blood of sleeping victims
- Can be destroyed by a stake through the heart.

What Will Happen To You Today?

- You will shed up to 100 hairs
- Your heart will beat about 100,000 times
- You will produce about 72 tablespoons of saliva
- You will create and destroy about 199.2 million blood cells
- You will inhale about 21,600 times
- You will produce about 120 tablespoons of urine
- You will produce about 65–200g (2–7oz) of poo
- You will fart about 14 times.

Five Ways To Tame A Troll

Tamed, a troll may bring you good luck and possibly a fortune. Untamed, a troll is likely to destroy things. There are some key signs to look out for if you suspect there's a troll in your garden. Most trolls turn to stone if the sun shines on them, so if you hear loud thudding noises just before dawn, this may be the sound of a troll scurrying to hide. If you notice long, wide footprints with eight toes in the flowerbeds, a troll is probably nearby. Read on to find out what to do.

Step one: feed your troll
Troll-taming is much easier if its stomach is full. Trolls are not fussy eaters, but slimy or rotten leftovers are best.

Step two: greet your troll
Smile and grunt to make your troll realize you are its friend. Point at yourself and say your name. Do this several times because trolls have small brains. Now point at your troll and raise your eyebrows. When your troll grunts its name, you're ready to move on.

Step three: give your troll a gift
Trolls have hooked noses that are often drippy – so your troll may find a handkerchief welcome. If your troll is one-eyed, it may appreciate an attractive eye-patch. Trolls love glowing treasure, so anything shiny will make them very happy.

Step four: treat your troll to a makeover

A very hairy troll – which many are – may enjoy a deep-conditioning hair treatment. If your troll has large horny toenails, why not pamper it with a pedicure? Some trolls have enormous bellies. If this is true of your troll, devise a fun fitness program you can tackle together.

Step five: accepting an invitation to your troll's home

If your troll beckons you to visit its cave or burrow, congratulations! Your troll is tamed. But remember, gasp with delight and clasp your hands as you enter its home. No matter how ghastly and smelly it seems to you, it is lovely to your troll. And it is never a good idea to upset a troll – even a tamed one.

Famous Vessels

Boats have been a part of human history for centuries, from the rowing vessels used by the ancient Egyptians to the huge cargo ships that sail the sea today. Here are some famous examples.

Queen Anne's Revenge
The famous pirate, Blackbeard, captured this French ship in 1717, and converted it into a 40-gun warship. It was used by Blackbeard to terrorize the Caribbean Sea. When he was finally captured and killed, his head was stuck on the end of the "bowsprit," a pole at the front of the ship.

Mary Celeste
In 1872, a mystery ship was found sailing in the north Atlantic with no one aboard, and no sign of what happened to the captain, his wife and small daughter, and the eight crew. Did they jump into lifeboats because their cargo of neat alcohol was about to explode? Was it mutiny? Piracy? An underwater earthquake? Or even an alien abduction? No one knows.

Titanic

The *Titanic* was a gigantic ocean liner, more than 269m (882ft) long with nine decks, and it was supposed to be unsinkable. It wasn't. On 14th April 1912, it hit an iceberg at 11.40 in the evening, and began to fill with water. Two hours and 40 minutes later, it sank. There weren't enough lifeboats for everyone on board, and many of them were launched only part full. More than 1,500 people died.

Kon-tiki

This raft was named after a legendary Inca god. In 1947, a Norwegian scientist, Thor Heyerdahl, and five crew sailed the raft across the Pacific Ocean. The team believed it was possible that ancient people from the west coast of South America could have made a similar journey to the Polynesian islands in the Pacific and colonized them (taken them over). Other people disagreed, and Thor wanted to prove his theory. The journey took three and a half months. They travelled 6,900km (4,300 miles). Today the raft is on display at a museum in Oslo, Norway.

The Number Three

Triceratops: a dinosaur with three horns – two large ones above its eyes and a smaller one on its snout.

Triathlon: a three-part race, involving swimming, cycling, and long-distance running.

Tricolore: the French three-colored flag.

Trigamist: a person who is married three times, or has three husbands or wives at once.

Tripod: a three-legged stand used to support things, such as cameras.

Triplets: three babies born at one birth.

Triennial: lasting three years, or happening every three years.

Tricorn: a hat with the brim turned up on three sides.

Tricycle: a three-wheeled-cycle.

More Number Three

Three wise men
- Melchior, King of Arabia (brought gold)
- Caspar, King of Tarsus (brought frankincense)
- Balthazar, King of Ethiopia (brought myrrh).

Three body types
- Endomorph (heavy, rounded build)
- Ectomorph (light, delicate build)
- Mesomorph (muscular build).

Three colors to mix
- Red and blue make purple
- Red and yellow make orange
- Blue and yellow make green.

Three ballets by a composer called Tchaikovsky
- Swan Lake
- The Nutcracker
- The Sleeping Beauty.

Three countries to first have TV
- UK (1936)
- USA (1939)
- USSR (1939).

Three musketeers
- Athos
- Porthos
- Aramis.

Three famous words
Veni, vidi, vici: I came, I saw, I conquered (said by Julius Caesar in 47BC after he won a small war in Pontus, an area in modern-day Turkey).

Letters Made Up Of Three Straight Lines

Triangles

Did you know that the study of triangles has its own name: trigonometry? Triangles can be grouped into three types.

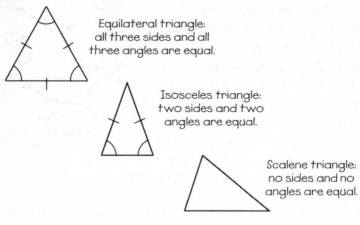

Equilateral triangle: all three sides and all three angles are equal.

Isosceles triangle: two sides and two angles are equal.

Scalene triangle: no sides and no angles are equal.

Sense-Sational: Sight

Your eye has millions of photoreceptors on its "retina," a soft transparent layer at the back of the eyeball. Photoreceptors see shapes and colors and send the information to the optic nerve, which is attached to the brain.

Eye muscles are the busiest muscles in your body, and are very strong. They react fast, and can contract (become tighter) in less than one hundredth of a second. This happens when your iris (the colored part of your eye) reacts to light. When there is a lot of light, the iris contracts to make the black pupil in the middle smaller. When it is darker, the iris opens the pupil, making it bigger to let in as much light as possible.

How To Confuse A Pigeon

The head of a pigeon contains tiny magnetic crystals that work by sensing the Earth's magnetic field, and help the bird to find its way home. To confuse a pigeon, simply tie a magnet to its head. The magnetic crystals in the pigeon's head will get thoroughly confused – and so will the pigeon. Obviously you would never want to try this because it would be mean. Really mean!

Lost pigeon

Some Tree Species To Spot

Alder	Cypress	Larch	Poplar
Ash	Elder	Maple	Rowan
Beech	Elm	Oak	Spruce
Birch	Eucalyptus	Palm	Sycamore
Cedar	Fir	Pine	Willow.
Chestnut	Hazel	Plane	

Fruit Trees

Apple	Grapefruit	Mango	Peach
Apricot	Guava	Mulberry	Pear
Cherry	Lemon	Orange	Plum
Fig	Lime	Papaya	Quince.

Amazing Trees

Trees are terrific, not least because they provide the oxygen you need to stay alive. Here are some of the tallest, weirdest, and wisest trees around.

Californian redwood

The tallest trees on Earth are giant redwoods, found in the Humboldt Redwood State Park, California, USA. They can take 400 years to mature, and some of the trees are thought to be more than 2,000 years old. The tallest giant redwood, named Hyperion, is 115.2m (378ft) tall. That's taller than the Statue of Liberty in New York, or the height of 26 double-decker buses piled on top of one another.

TREE-MENDOUS!

Baobab

The baobab, or "upside down tree" as it is also known, wins the award for weirdest tree. Found in Africa, the baobab has a wide, fat, knobbly trunk shaped like a barrel.

The tree's nickname comes from its spreading root-like branches, which make it look like it's been pulled out of the ground and stuck back in upside-down.

Banyan tree

The banyan is not as silly as it may look – it's actually a very smart tree. It sends shoots, lots of them, down from its branches. The shoots all take root in the ground, and become new trunks, which then repeat the same process.

One super-smart specimen in Kolkata, India, has managed to grow about 230 very big trunks and 3,000 smaller ones. That's one clever tree!

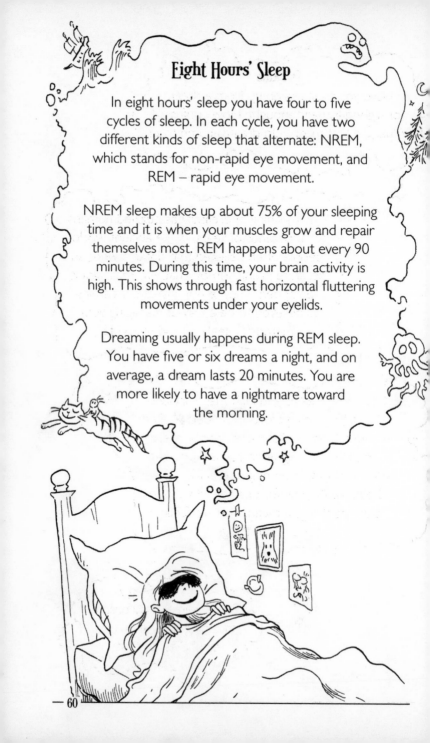

Eight Hours' Sleep

In eight hours' sleep you have four to five cycles of sleep. In each cycle, you have two different kinds of sleep that alternate: NREM, which stands for non-rapid eye movement, and REM – rapid eye movement.

NREM sleep makes up about 75% of your sleeping time and it is when your muscles grow and repair themselves most. REM happens about every 90 minutes. During this time, your brain activity is high. This shows through fast horizontal fluttering movements under your eyelids.

Dreaming usually happens during REM sleep. You have five or six dreams a night, and on average, a dream lasts 20 minutes. You are more likely to have a nightmare toward the morning.

Dreams

Have you ever woken up from a dream (or nightmare) and thought: How confusing! What did that mean? Do dreams come true?

The meaning of dreams has puzzled humans for thousands of years. In the ancient world, people often believed that dreams were an accurate prediction of what was really going to happen. They're not. Instead, dreaming is believed to be a way of managing your memories, feelings, and thoughts.

Common dreams and nightmares include flying, falling, being chased, and being naked in public. If you feel stressed in your dream, this may be a sign that you are feeling anxious about something in real life. If your dream is positive (for example, if you are enjoying flying) it means you are feeling good about things.

Some animals also dream, including dogs, monkeys, elephants, and rats.

Reasons To Close Your Mouth At Night

Spiders • Cockroaches • Mosquitoes • Dust • Beetles
• Fleas • Earwigs • Waking up with a dry mouth

Foot Binding

The practice of foot binding began in China around 960BC. It was a cruel tradition, done to stop girls' feet growing more than 7.5–10cm (3–4in) long. Small feet were considered beautiful – and it was thought that they made women's movements dainty and feminine.

The process was long and extremely painful. The toenails of infant girls were clipped, and their feet were soaked in hot water and herbs, or sometimes urine or warm animal blood. Once the tissue and bones were softened, the feet were massaged and covered with special salts, called alum.

All toes (except for the big toes) were then broken and folded under the sole of each foot. The toes were bound in place with a long silk or cotton bandage. The bandages were removed every two days so that the toes could be washed and the nails clipped to avoid infection. The bandages were put back on and gradually made tighter and tighter.

Eventually the arch of each foot was broken, and the foot was pulled straight down. The size of girls' shoes reduced as their feet shrank. The process took about two years to complete, after which the bandages were only removed to wash the feet. Foot binding was banned in 1912, but the practice continued in secret for many years after that.

Hairstyles

Beehive

Corkscrew curls

Dreadlocks

French braid

Quiff

Cornrows

Bob

Finger wave

Pigtails

Mohawk

Earthquake Legends

Scientists will tell you that earthquakes are caused by shifts in the plates that form the Earth's crust. But in past times, people had different ideas about the cause of earthquakes.

Central America
The Chorotegra people, who were originally from Mexico, believed that the Earth was one big flat square, with a god standing on each corner. If the gods thought the Earth was getting too full of people, they'd give it a tip to make some of the people fall off – a simple solution.

West Africa
This legend probably originated from a group called the Fon people, who lived in West Africa. They believed that the Earth was flat. One side was held up by a mountain, and the other was held up by a giant. The giant's wife held up the sky

I'D MOVE MOUNTAINS FOR YOU, MY LOVE.

and, if the giant was in a particularly cheeky mood, he gave her a hug, which made the Earth tremble. Talk about being distracted by love!

Siberia

The people of Kamchatka in Siberia, Russia, thought that the Earth moved around the Universe on a huge sled driven by the god Tuli, and pulled by dogs. Sometimes the dogs had to stop and give themselves a good scratch to get rid of fleas, which shook the Earth. If only flea treatments had been invented, just think how easy it would have been to prevent earthquakes.

· ·

What To Do In An Earthquake

· ·

If you are unlucky enough to be around when an earthquake hits, here is some useful advice you should remember.

Indoors: Find shelter as far inside the building as possible – head for lower floors with plenty of exits. Stay away from windows that might shatter. Avoid objects that could fall on you and find a sturdy piece of furniture to shelter beneath. If you can't shelter under furniture, crouch in an inside corner of a room and cover your face and head with your hands.

Outdoors: Keep away from tall buildings. If you are on a hillside, head for the top, as there may be a landslide. In coastal areas avoid cliffs and, after the quake, head for high ground in case of tidal waves. Lie flat on the ground, and if debris flies past you, curl yourself into a tight ball. Beware of aftershocks (smaller earthquakes that happen after the main one). They can be as destructive as the original.

A Brief History Of Pens

1. Around 4000BC: Ancient Egyptians used thin-stemmed reed brushes to write on "papyrus" (a material made from strips of a reed-like plant).

2. Ancient Greeks and Romans used wax tablets and scratched letters on them with a wooden or iron stick called a stylus.

3. Around 500–300BC: Ancient Greeks refined the reed pen by introducing a split nib to channel ink.

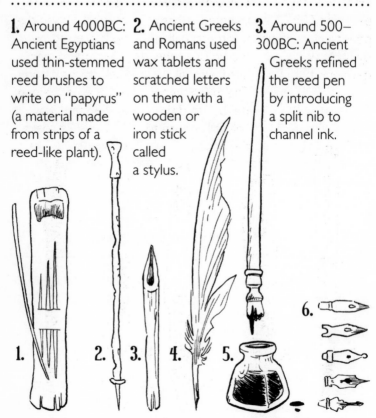

1.   **2.**   **3.**   **4.**   **5.**   **6.**

4. Romans developed quill pens made from the wing-feathers of large birds. For centuries, these were the most widely used writing instruments.

5. 1830s: Steel-nib pens began to replace quill pens. They were expensive, as the nibs were handmade.

6. 1850s: "Screw press" machines stamped out nib shapes from steel. All pens were dipped in ink pots to write.

7. Around 1880–1900: Fountain pens, the first pens to store their own ink, were developed.

8. 1938: The ballpoint pen was invented. It has a tiny metal ball in the tip of a tube filled with ink. The ink sticks to the ball, and the ball rolls ink on to the paper.

9. 1962: The fiber-tip pen was created. When the tip is pressed on paper, the paper sucks the ink from a supply in the pen, in the same way as a sponge soaks up water.

7.

8.

9.

10.

11.

10. 1966: The rollerball pen was developed, with a metal ball like the ballpoint and the ink supply of a fibre-tip pen.

11. 1979: Erasable-ink pens were created. The pen's ink can be rubbed out, but becomes "indelible" (meaning it can't be removed) after a day or two.

Today there are pens for all sorts of writing needs – astronauts use special space pens that can write while they are upside down.

The Greek Alphabet

The Greek alphabet was developed in Greece around 1000BC. It has 24 letters, and you will probably come across some of them when you study math and science. Here they all are in the correct order.

Look closely at the first two letters – *alpha* and *beta*. This is where the word "alphabet" comes from, when the two words are combined.

Six Rules For Sparkling Teeth

1. Never skip tooth-brushing. Brush your teeth up and down, front and back, twice a day for at least two minutes.

2. Your tongue can trap particles of food and bacteria, so it's important to brush your tongue, too.

3. Use dental floss to get rid of any food or plaque trapped between your teeth.

4. Do a final brush or use a mouthwash to rinse out any bits of food you cleared out while flossing.

5. Drink water after you eat to help wash any bacteria in your mouth down into your stomach.

6. Snack on raw vegetables, not sugary sweet things.

In Vermont, a law says women must get written permission from their husbands to wear false teeth.

HOLD ON DEAR, JUST NEED TO SIGN IT ...

Greek And Roman Goddesses

Ancient Greeks and Romans believed their worlds were ruled by gods and goddesses, who were linked to different aspects of nature and human life. The goddesses were the same, but the Greeks and the Romans called them by different names.

Goddess of	Greek goddess	Roman goddess
Truth	Alethia	Veritas
Beauty and love	Aphrodite	Venus
Hunting	Artemis	Diana
Wisdom and war	Athena	Minerva
Fertility and crops	Demeter	Ceres
Dawn	Eos	Aurora
Discord, strife (disagreement)	Eris	Discordia
The Earth	Gaea	Tellus
Youth	Hebe	Juventas
Marriage	Hera	Juno
Home and hearth	Hestia	Vesta
Victory	Nike	Victoria
Spring	Persephone	Proserpina
Moon	Selene	Luna

In 320AD the Roman Emperor, Constantinus I and the Catholic Church banned sausages and made sausage-eating a sin.

Things You Don't Want To Be Your Friend

A werewolf is a creature who is possibly the perfect friend by day, but not by night – especially during a full moon – as he turns into a monstrous, extremely hairy, girl-eating wolf thing. A werewolf has eyebrows that meet in the middle, fangs instead of teeth, claws instead of fingers, and different colored eyes … not a good look.

Gargantua is a giant described in a collection of French novels, published in the 1500s. He is prone to opening his mouth so wide when he is sleeping that passing armies fall into it. He is French (so has a dreamy accent) but don't be fooled – he is known to take humans, including girls, prisoner and wedge them in a gap between his teeth.

A Girl's Guide To Choosing A Dog

The perfect pooch is one who matches your style and personality. But beware: some people say owners end up looking like their dogs!

1. Chihuahua: A teeny weeny dog with a big personality. The chihuahua is easily carried if you are in a rush, making it ideal for the busy girl on the go.

2. Afghan hound: The Afghan hound likes plenty of exercise, and would be perfect for a sporty girl.

3. Pug: This dog has a grumpy-looking face and a weirdly curled tail – best for girls with a sense of humor.

4. Poodle: A quirky choice, a poodle is a brainy dog ideal for the girl with a kooky sense of style.

5. Bulldog: This dog is not clever and not pretty – but it is strong. For girls who know that looks aren't everything.

6. Pekingese: A very hairy pooch, with a flat face, a broad snout, and an extremely snooty expression. A Pekingese would suit a girl with attitude.

7. Great Dane: An extremely large dog, probably best for girls who live in a mansion, with a park-sized garden.

8. German shepherd: This intelligent dog may cause nervous girls to have nightmares, as it looks scarily like a wolf. Best for fearless females.

9. Dachshund: Also known as the sausage dog, the dachshund has short legs and a long body. It is playful, but also stubborn. Suited to the girl who doesn't like long walks.

10. Dalmatian: A gorgeously spotty dog. Dalmatians are known for tirelessly running long distances, and would make a good partner for the girl who is training for a marathon.

Endangered Animals

A species of animal becomes endangered when there are so few of them left that they might soon disappear altogether. These are just some endangered animals:

Mammals

- African wild dog
- Asian elephant
- Bactrian camel
- Blue whale
- Cheetah
- Giant armadillo
- Giant panda
- Maned three-toed sloth
- Northern hairy-nosed wombat
- Orangutan
- Polar bear
- Snow leopard

Birds

- Black robin
- California condor
- Chestnut-bellied hummingbird
- Crowned eagle
- Egyptian vulture
- Galapagos penguin
- Ivory-bellied woodpecker
- Oriental stork
- Purple-backed sunbeam
- Red siskin
- Whooping crane

Amphibians and reptiles

- American crocodile
- Bermuda rock lizard
- Blue-sided tree frog
- Bog turtle
- Californian tiger salamander
- Caucasian viper
- Egyptian tortoise
- Komodo dragon
- Leaf-nosed lizard
- Ornamental snake
- Painted terrapin
- Scarlet harlequin toad
- Spotted turtle.

Well-Known Dishes From Around The World

Every country has a dish (or several) that it is famous for eating. Here is a selection to tuck into.

Australia: Australians are known for doing a mean barbecue. Grilled shrimp is a particular speciality.

Japan: Sushi (pronounced *soo-she*) is a popular Japanese dish of small, cold, rice rolls with fillings, including fresh raw fish.

France: Bouillabaisse (*bu-ee-ya-base*) is a hearty fish soup, eaten with "baguette" (a crusty French bread) on the side.

Spain: Paella (pronounced *pie-ee-ya*) consists of rice simmered with shrimp, mussels, chicken, and spices.

Italy: Pizza is a flat, round bread that is oven-baked and topped with various ingredients. It originated in Naples, Italy, but today pizza is eaten around the world.

Poltergeists

Some people believe in poltergeists, noisy and mischievous spirits that haunt houses with children and teenagers in them. Here are ten telltale signs to look out for if you suspect a poltergeist is around:

1. Pictures flying off the walls and across the room
2. Objects being hurled to the floor by invisible hands
3. Loud knocking noises
4. Creepy singing
5. Echoing footsteps
6. Sudden icy breezes
7. Slamming doors
8. Chattering voices in empty rooms
9. A piano that starts to play by itself
10. Cats hissing for no reason.

In A Heartbeat

- A gray whale's heart averages nine beats per minute.
- A healthy human heart averages 60–100 beats per minute.
- A hummingbird's heart averages 1,200 beats per minute.

Most Active Animals At Night

Aardvark • Badger • Bat • Hippopotamus • Koala • Lion • Mink • Mole • Otter • Owl • Panda • Tiger • Skunk

The Buttered Cat Paradox

If buttered toast always lands buttered side down and a cat always lands on its feet, what would happen if you attached a buttered piece of toast, butter-side up, to a cat's back and threw them both from a great height?

Animal Antics

The animal kindgdom is a weird and wonderful place. Did you know that:

- A snail can sleep for three years.
- Queen ants sleep on average nine hours a day, while poor worker ants have to grab what they can get by taking hundreds of short power naps.
- A mole can dig a tunnel 90m (295ft) long in one night.
- Slugs have one large foot and this is the part of the body that moves them along.
- Giraffes have tongues that are over a foot long.

All's Not Well

William Shakespeare wrote some of the world's best-known plays and poems. Here are the tragic plots of two of his love stories.

Romeo and Juliet

The Montagues and Capulets, two powerful families, are feuding. Romeo (a Montague) attends a Capulet ball in disguise, and he and Juliet (a Capulet) fall in love.

They marry in secret the next day, helped by Friar Laurence. However Tybalt, Juliet's cousin, is angry that Romeo came to the party uninvited and challenges him to fight. When Romeo refuses, his friend Mercutio fights instead. Tybalt kills Mercutio, so Romeo kills Tybalt in revenge and is banished.

Juliet's family, who still have no idea that she is now married, want her to marry her cousin, Paris. Friar Laurence gives Juliet a potion to fake her own death, making her appear dead for two days. He tries to send a message to Romeo so that he can secretly rescue Juliet from her tomb, but Romeo doesn't get the message.

When Romeo returns and hears Juliet is dead, he comes to her tomb, kills Paris, kisses Juliet, then takes poison and dies. Juliet wakes, sees Romeo is dead, and stabs herself. The families decide to end their feud, but it's too late for poor Romeo and Juliet. A truly tragic tale.

Antony and Cleopatra

Mark Antony is a great soldier and one of three rulers of Rome. He falls in love with Cleopatra, the Queen of Egypt.

Antony is married to a woman called Fulvia. News reaches him in Egypt that Fulvia has died, so Antony returns to Rome and marries the sister of Octavius, another ruler of Rome. Relations between Octavius and Antony have been tense, and the marriage is intended to smooth things over. Cleopatra is jealous when she hears the news.

Antony can't resist going back to Cleopatra in Egypt. When Octavius hears of this, he declares war on Egypt. (So much for smoothing things over.) Octavius and Antony fight a battle at sea. Cleopatra goes with Antony to the battle, but her presence causes a military disaster. Antony is defeated.

Fighting continues and things get complicated. Antony thinks Cleopatra is plotting against him with Octavius, which she isn't. Angry at the accusation, Cleopatra goes into hiding and sends Antony false news that she is dead. Hearing the news, Antony stabs himself and is taken, dying, to Cleopatra. Antony dies in her arms and, overcome by grief, Cleopatra lets a poisonous snake bite her. This time she dies – for real.

Sense-Sational: Smell

Smells are particles, too small to be seen. As you inhale, you draw them into your nose. There, they are picked up by millions of nerve endings, which relay the information to the brain. Your brain tells you what is being smelled.

Your nose can sniff out seven main smells:
- rose-scented (flowers)
- minty (chewing gum)
- musky (perfume)
- camphoric (mothballs)
- pungent (vinegar)
- ethereal (cleaning fluid)
- putrid (rotting eggs).

All other smells are made from these seven smells mixed together in different amounts and combinations. Your nose can tell the difference between about 10,000 different smells. Your granny has a worse sense of smell than you do. Your dog has a much better sense of smell – but a lot less brain.

Mighty Mountain

Olympus Mons, on the planet Mars, is an enormous volcano – the biggest mountain in our Solar System. It measures up to 624km (388 miles) across and rises approximately 25km (16 miles) above the surface of the planet, making it three times as high as Mount Everest, the tallest mountain on Earth.

For Your Address Book

Here are some useful contacts for your address book:

Mr and Mrs Dursley
4 Privet Drive,
Little Whinging,
Surrey, Great Britain

FAO: Batman
Wayne Manor
Gotham City,
USA

Sherlock Holmes
221b Baker Street,
London

Peter Pan
Second to the right
and then straight on
till morning,
Neverland

AIR MAIL
Bart Simpson
742 Evergreen Terrace,
Springfield, USA

Santa
The
North Pole

Excellent Excuses

Imagine finding yourself in these four tricky situations. You could say sorry – or you could use one of these handy excuses.

1. You shut your annoying little brother in his wardrobe, just as your mom walks in:

"I was demonstrating the difference between fact and fiction books, by showing him his wardrobe is not a magic gateway to a faraway land."

2. Your dad finds you stuffing your face with candy just before dinner.

"I'm considering a career in the confectionery industry, and I'm getting to know the products so I can speak knowledgeably at interviews."

3. You doze off during a long, boring biology class and your teacher spots you:

"I wasn't asleep. I was briefly hibernating, which is something many small mammals do in winter."

4. Your friend's mom spots you hiding her disgusting dinner in your purse to throw away later.

"It's so delicious I want my mom to taste it, too. Please can I take the recipe so we can make it at home?"

Future Events That Will Be Worth Watching

- The first contact between humans and aliens
- The launch of the first package holiday to the Moon
- The first demonstration of real magic
- The launch of invisibility potions in supermarkets
- The discovery that dinosaurs are not extinct, just hiding.

Spiders – The Facts

Do you love spiders or does the sight of them make your skin crawl? Maybe you will like them more when you find out these eight-legged creatures are quite remarkable.

Spiders use silk thread to spin their webs. Spider silk is an oozy liquid that turns into thread when it hits the air. The thread can be thin, thick, sticky, or slippery and is not just for webs. Spiders also use it to make "cocoons" (protective cases) or lifelines if they have to suddenly jump from somewhere tall – handy.

Spiders make more than one kind of web. Orb webs are circular, spinning out from the center like spokes on a wheel. Sheet webs are a favorite with forest spiders, and look a bit like hammocks (although you wouldn't want to lie in one). Triangle webs are spun between two forked branches, or the crooks of trees, and tangle webs, as the name suggests, are not neat, but they are effective for catching flies.

Spiders' webs are protein-packed, and a really hungry spider sometimes eats its own web. Gross! There's no danger of being caught in their own traps though, because spiders have oily toes to stop them getting stuck.

"ARACHNOPHOBIA" IS A FEAR OF SPIDERS.

Amazing Sisters

Talented writers

Charlotte, Emily, and Anne Brontë were talented novelists. They grew up in a bleak, isolated village in the Yorkshire moors in England. The sisters had a hard upbringing and their early experiences had a great influence on their haunting writing styles. By 1847, all three had published a novel. Charlotte and Emily wrote two very famous books – *Jane Eyre* (by Charlotte Brontë) and *Wuthering Heights* (by Emily Brontë).

Showbiz sensations

Kylie and Dannii Minogue are two sisters from Australia. Kylie started acting when she was a child and went on to become a world-famous pop singer. Her sister Dannii also acted when she was young before going on to have a singing career. More recently Dannii has been a judge on the UK *X Factor* and *Australia's Got Talent,* and she has her own fashion label.

Tennis champions

Serena and Venus Williams are world-class tennis champions. The sisters were introduced to tennis at the age of five by their father, and in 2002, they became the first siblings ever to occupy the first and second positions in the world tennis-rankings (meaning they were classified as the top two women tennis players in the world at that time).

Simpson sisters

Patty and Selma Bouvier are fictional twin sisters from the cartoon, *The Simpsons*. Born in 1947, they are Marge Simpson's older sisters. They both hold a strong dislike of Marge's husband, Homer.

Zodiac Signs

Aries
21 March – 19 April

Taurus
20 April – 20 May

Gemini
21 May – 21 June

Cancer
22 June – 22 July

Leo
23 July – 22 Aug.

Virgo
23 Aug. – 22 Sept.

Libra
23 Sept. – 23 Oct.

Scorpio
24 Oct. – 21 Nov.

Sagittarius
22 Nov. – 21 Dec.

Capricorn
22 Dec. – 19 Jan.

Aquarius
20 Jan. – 18 Feb.

Pisces
19 Feb.– 20 March

Ballet Terms

Have you ever heard people talk about the perfect "pirouette" or a beautiful "pas de deux" but never had a clue what they are talking about? Help is at hand. Many ballet terms come from the French language. Here are a few basic ones with their meanings.

Cambré: A bend from the waist.

Enchaînement: A series of steps linked together in sequence (meaning they follow each other in a particular order).

Entrechat: A jump where the dancer's legs criss-cross in the air.

Fouetté: A whipping move of the leg, often to create momentum to perform a turn or jump.

Jeté: A basic ballet step – a jump from one foot to the other, similar to a leap.

Pas de deux: Meaning "step of two," a dance for two people.

Pirouette: A complete turn, or series of turns, on one leg – literal translation is "to whirl."

Plié: bending of the knees.

Relevé: Translates as "lifted." This move involves rising up off the heels.

Sauté: Jumping off both feet, landing in the same position.

Ballet Positions

There are five basic foot positions in ballet, and every basic move begins and ends with one of these positions. The positions were established by a French ballet dancer called Pierre Beauchamp in the late 17th century.

Third

Second

Fourth

First

Fifth

Famous Ballets

Cinderella • Coppélia • Don Quixote • Firebird • Giselle • La Bayadère (The Temple Dancer) • Sleeping Beauty

A Dessert Named After A Ballerina: Pavlova

Pavlova is a summery dessert inspired by a Russian ballerina called Anna Matveyevna Pavlova (1881–1931). It is supposed to be as light and delicate as Pavlova herself, who was said to soar "as though on wings."

You will need:
For the meringue: 3 egg whites
• 175g (¾ cup) caster sugar (superfine sugar).

For the topping: 284ml (1 cup) double cream (whipped)
• 450g (3 cups) mixed berries (e.g. raspberries, strawberries, blackberries) • 1 tbsp powdered sugar.

1. Turn on the oven to Gas Mark 4/180°C/350°F.

2. Place a large plate on a sheet of baking paper and draw around it. Turn the paper over and place on a large baking tray, making sure it covers the tray completely. Put to one side.

3. Separate the egg whites into a large mixing bowl.

4. Ask an adult to use an electric beater to whisk the egg whites until the mixture starts to thicken.

5. Gradually add the sugar to the mixing bowl, whisking all the time until the mixture stands up in stiff, shiny peaks.

6. When you can turn the bowl upside down and the mixture doesn't move it is ready. This will take around 8–10 minutes of beating.

7. Spoon the mixture on to the covered baking tray. Use the circle outline on the baking paper as a guide. Starting in the middle of the circle, use the back of a large spoon or a rubber spatula to smooth the mixture so it fills the shape of the circle.

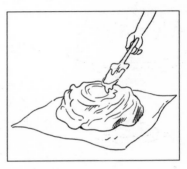

8. Turn the oven down to Gas Mark ½/120°C/250°F . Ask an adult to bake the meringue in the oven for 1½ hours.

9. Tap the bottom of the meringue, and if it makes a crisp sound it is ready. Once cooked, leave the meringue inside the oven until it is completely cold.

10. Carefully peel the pavlova off the parchment and transfer it to a serving dish. Spoon the whipped cream over the pavlova, and then add the fruit on top. Dust with the powdered sugar. Dig in!

WARNING: ALWAYS ASK AN ADULT TO HELP YOU WHEN YOU USE THE OVEN.

Five Ways To Find A Mate

In the animal kingdom some males will go to great lengths to get their girl.

1. A male spotted bowerbird tries to impress the ladies with a stylish pad. He builds a U-shaped bower from dried grasses and decorates it with treasures he's picked up – the more shiny and colorful the better. Great care is taken to arrange the items symmetrically, and in such a way that they will reflect the sunlight. Treasures that have been found in nests include all sorts of things.

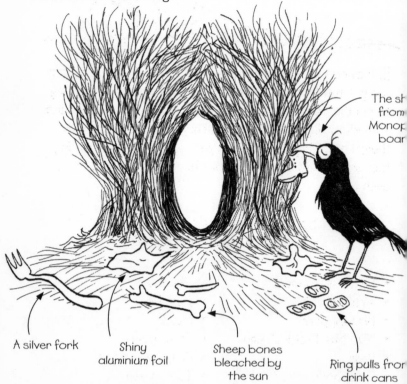

The sh
from
Monop
boar

A silver fork

Shiny
aluminium foil

Sheep bones
bleached by
the sun

Ring pulls fror
drink cans

2. Male newts show off their sensitive sides with carefully choreographed water ballets.

3. Male dance flies know the way to a girl's heart is through her stomach, and bring her gifts of freshly killed insects.

4. A male rainbow lizard wows the ladies by turning his head bright red, then does push-ups to show he's in tip-top condition.

5. If all else fails, many male animals fight each other to get the girl. Rattlesnakes wrestle for up to an hour, each trying to pin the other's head to the ground. Dolphins are childish – head-butting, biting, and scratching the rival's skin with their teeth. Elephant seals can get so carried away fighting they sometimes crush little pups beneath them and don't even notice!

....

Strange Things People Collect
....

- Pencil-sharpeners
- Artificial apples
- Nail-clippers
- "Do Not Disturb" signs
- Bells
- Teaspoons
- Sick-bags
- Candles
- Masks
- Telephones
- Belly-button fluff
- Toothpaste.

Number Seven

Seven things that are made up of seven things.

The seven dwarves in Disney's film Snow White
Bashful • Doc • Dopey • Grumpy • Happy • Sleepy • Sneezy

And seven names that weren't used
Blabby • Crabby • Dizzy • Gloomy • Jaunty • Lazy • Shifty

The seven wonders of the ancient world
The Colossus of Rhodes • The Pyramids of Giza • The Hanging Gardens of Babylon • The Pharos of Alexandria • The Mausoleum of Halicarnassus • The Statue of Zeus at Olympia • The Temple of Artemis at Ephesus

The seven natural wonders of the world
The Grand Canyon (USA) • The Great Barrier Reef (Australia) • The Harbor of Rio de Janeiro (Brazil) • Mount Everest (Nepal) • The Northern Lights, also known as Aurora Borealis (the Arctic Circle) • Paricutin Volcano (Mexico) • Victoria Falls (Zambia)

The seven deadly sins
Pride • greed • lust • envy • gluttony • anger • sloth

The seven key functions of all living things
Movement • sensitivity • respiration • nutrition • growth • reproduction • excretion

The seven events that make up the women's heptathlon
100-meter hurdles • high jump • shot put • 200-meter run • long jump • javelin throw • 800-mete run

Cool Dreams To Have About School

Terrified teachers
Dreaming you turn invisible on the way to assembly, and run around the auditorium wailing, so everyone thinks the school is haunted.

Sudden stardom
Dreaming you get to school and find that your math test is canceled because your favorite boy band are filming their next video in your classroom and they want you to star in it.

Incredible ice cream
Dreaming that the lunch ladies have put magic ice cream on the menu that tastes of different flavors with every mouthful – delicious!

Dino dream
Dreaming the school bus takes you through time one Monday morning to go dinosaur spotting – fun *and* educational.

Things You Don't Want To Meet In The Park

Barghest is an enormous dog, with horns, fangs, and fiery eyes, who inflicts terrible wounds that never heal. In Yorkshire, England, it is said that spotting Barghest is a bad omen that means something even ghastlier than meeting it is likely to happen to you quite soon.

Cerberus is a monstrous and vicious dog with three heads from Greek mythology. Snake heads grow from his back and he has a serpent's tail. Cerberus guards the entrance to Hades, the Greek underworld, so he will be lost (and probably extremely angry) if spotted in your local park.

Peculiar Plants

Some common plant names are pretty peculiar. If only "Big Money" was a plant that money actually grew on.

- Sneezewort
- Kangaroo paw
- Monkey puzzle
- Brown turkey
- Big ears
- Bleeding heart
- Swiss cheese plant
- Devil's tobacco
- Sailor caps

- Custard plant
- Spoon flower
- Giant dogwood
- Mugwort
- Caulescent red-hot poker
- Big money
- Fairy elephant's feet
- Blue horizon

- Painted fingernail
- Flying tiger
- Pheasant's eye
- Green thumb
- Lamb's tail
- Monk's hood
- Nana
- Wisley jester
- Balloon flower.

Types Of Footwear

Slipper

Flip-flop

Rain boot

Wedge

Stiletto heel

Kitten heel

Slingback

Brogue

Sneaker

Cowboy boot

Wooden clog

Moccasin

Say It With Flowers

Did you know that flowers have their own secret language? Different blooms carry different meanings, so why not build the ultimate bouquet for your mom or your BFF to express just how much she means to you?

Pink carnation: I will never forget you

Crocus: Youth and happiness

Oak-leaved geranium: True friendship

Gardenia: Joy

Honeysuckle: Devotion

Hyacinth: Playfulness

White lily: Sweetness

Tall sunflower: Appreciation

Pink rose: Friendship

Bluebell: Reliability

Larkspur: Laughter

Dandelion: Wisdom

Lupin: Imagination

Fuchsia: Good taste

Purple pansy: You are in my thoughts.

I Love You

Next time you write a love letter, you can impress the person you are sending it to by signing it off in several different languages. It will definitely get their attention (and you may even win their heart!).

Je t'aime (French)
Ich liebe dich (German)
Te amo (Spanish)
Ti amo (Italian)
Ik hou van je (Dutch)
Minä rakastan sinua (Finnish)
Kocham cie (Polish)
Eu te amo (Portuguese)

Ya tebya lyublyu (Russian)
Jag älskar dig (Swedish)
Seni seviyorum (Turkish)
Aishiteru (Japanese)

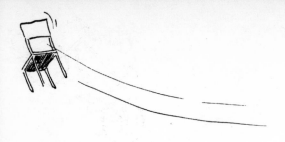

Hair-Raising

The Beaufort scale is used to measure wind strength. It was invented in 1805 by Francis Beaufort, an officer in the British Navy, as a way of observing how strong the wind was at sea. Today it is useful for looking at the behavior of wind across a large area, but what a girl really needs to know is how it will affect her hair.

Beaufort number	Wind description	Hair impact
0	Calm	Hair remains still
1	Light air	Hair quivers gently
2	Light breeze	Hair quivers more
3	Gentle breeze	Hair begins to sway
4	Moderate breeze	Hair sways more vigorously
5	Fresh breeze	Hair starts swishing
6	Strong breeze	Hair whips around face
7	Near gale	Hair makes slapping motions across cheeks
8	Gale	Hair becomes horribly messy
9	Severe gale	Hair resembles bird's nest
10	Storm	Considerable damage to hair
11	Violent storm	Hair beyond help
12	Hurricane	Stop worrying about your hair and seek shelter immediately!

How To Do A Bun

A bun is the perfect hairstyle for every girl out and about in a wind of force 5 and above. It works best on medium-length to long hair.

1. Brush your hair well, then go through it with a comb to check it's free of tangles.

2. Tie a ponytail wherever you want your bun to be, then comb it to make sure it's really smooth.

3. Twist your ponytail into a tight rope of hair.

4. Wrap the rope of hair round your ponytail base, twisting it more if you need to.

5. Tuck the ends of the hair neatly under the bun and into the ponytail base.

6. Use bobby pins to secure the bun.

7. Give your hairstyle a light squirt of hairspray to fix it.

The Echidna

The echidna is a mammal that can be found in Australia, Tasmania, and New Guinea. It's nicknamed the spiny anteater because its body is covered in long spines. Apart from the platypus, it is the only mammal that lays eggs rather than giving birth to its young. Echidnas are among the oldest mammals on Earth – the oldest known echidna fossil is about 17 million years old. A baby echidna is called a puggle. Cute!

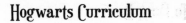

Hogwarts Curriculum

Imagine if you were a student at
Hogwarts School of Witchcraft
and Wizardry. Going to school
would never be boring, and
having Harry Potter in your
class would be pretty cool.
Here is a list of the subjects you
would have to study, and the
grades you could get.

Core subjects studied:
Charms
History of Magic
Transfiguration
Defense Against the
Dark Arts
Potions
Astronomy
Herbology

Options:
Arithmancy
Ancient Runes
Divination
Care of Magical
Creatures
Muggle Studies

The Ordinary Wizarding Levels (O.W.L.s) grading system:

Pass grades:
O = Outstanding
E = Exceeds expectations
A = Acceptable

Fail grades:
P = Poor
D = Dreadful
T = Troll

Horse Breeds

For centuries people have bred different kinds of horses. Here are a few examples.

Akhal-Teke	Fjord	Mustang
American paint	Gelderlander	Palomino
American quarter	Haflinger	Selle Français
Andalusian	Holsteiner	Shire
Appaloosa	Icelandic	Suffolk punch
Arabian	Irish draught	Tennessee walking
Carmargue	Knabstrupper	Tersk
Cleveland bay	Lippizaner	Thoroughbred
Clydesdale	Lusitano	Trakehner.
Dutch warmblood	Morgan	

Pony Breeds

A pony is a breed of small horse that is under 147cm (58in) tall. Here are a few examples.

Burmese	Exmoor	Java
Connemara	Fell	New Forest
Dales	French Saddle	Shetland
Dartmoor	Highland	Welsh Mountain.

Horse Colors

Bay	Brown	Cremello	Piebald
Black	Buckskin	Dun	Roan
Brindle	Chestnut	Palomino	Skewbald.

How To Act Perfectly Posh At A Banquet

If you are lucky enough to be invited to a lavish banquet at an enormous, fancy house, here are some top tips to make sure you sparkle, survive – and enjoy – the evening.

- Slouching is a ghastly error, so make sure you sit up straight. If it helps, pretend to balance an invisible book on your head.

- A napkin is for your lap, not for tucking round your neck, so resist the urge.

- Cutlery should be used in order, starting from the outside and working in.

- Soup-slurping is a definite no-no.

- Elbows should be by your sides as you eat. Pretend you have two more invisible books, one popped under each arm.

- Laugh loudly, yet daintily, at your host's jokes – even if they're not funny.

- The weather is a good topic of conversation. What weird and hairy things feet can be is a bad topic of conversation.

Sense-Sational: Hearing

Ears can be big or small, stick out or lie flat, but their main function is for hearing. So listen up!

Sounds are made when something moves or vibrates. Sound vibrations travel through the air at a speed of 343m (1,125ft 5in) per second. By trapping these sounds, your ears relay information to your brain about the type of sound and where it is coming from.

Sound is measured in decibels and anything above 130 decibels (dB) might start to be painful. Listening to anything louder than 90dB for a long period of time can damage your hearing, and a noise of 185dB would burst your eardrums. Here are some average decibel levels:

A plane taking off ⋯⋯⋯⋯⋯⋯⋯⋯⋯ 30–140dB
A vacuum cleaner ⋯⋯⋯⋯⋯⋯⋯⋯ up to 90dB
A normal conversation ⋯⋯⋯⋯⋯⋯⋯ 60dB
A whisper ⋯⋯⋯⋯⋯⋯⋯⋯⋯⋯⋯⋯ 20–30dB
Leaves rustling ⋯⋯⋯⋯⋯⋯⋯⋯⋯⋯ 10–20dB.

Things That Come In Twos

- Salt and pepper
- Bucket and spade
- Hansel and Gretel
- Beauty and the Beast
- Bread and butter
- Thunder and lightning
- Bella and Edward
- Batman and Robin
- Knife and fork
- Night and day
- Hide and seek
- Fish and chips.

Braille

Braille is a system of writing and printing for the blind. It uses patterns of raised dots to represent all the letters of the alphabet. It was invented by Louis Braille (1809–1852). Louis became blind after an accident with a tool in his father's workshop at the age of three. He started developing Braille when he was only 15. In this example, the black dots represent the raised dots. Can you can spell your name using the Braille alphabet?

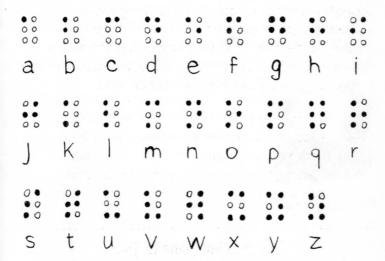

Sales of the bra may have been helped by the First World War. In 1917, the US Navy asked women to stop buying corsets, which had metal in them. Women did stop, and that freed up 28,000 tons of metal, which was enough for the navy to build two battleships.

Suffering For Fashion

Throughout history women have followed some freaky fashions, and endured extreme discomfort, all in the name of looking good.

Hair-raising

In the 18th century, the French nobility favoured the "Pompadour" hairstyle. Women stuck cages on their heads, and smoothed hair over them. They added small decorations, like ribbons, feathers, or flowers, or sometimes very big details, such as model boats, complete with sails, flags – and cannons. The hair didn't get washed for months, meaning it was not unknown for a lady to discover she had a head full of lice, or other vermin, when she did wash it.

Pale and poisonous

In the 16th century, Queen Elizabeth I of England liked to cover her blemishes with thick white make-up. And where queens lead, the ladies of the royal court all follow. Unfortunately, the make-up contained lead which, for some unlucky ladies, destroyed their skin and poisoned them.

Silly shoes

In the 1960s and 1970s it was really fashionable to wear platform shoes. In the 21st century, shoes have gone to new heights, with some designers, such as Alexander McQueen, showing shoes with towering heels. Watch your step!

Tight fit

Fashionable 19th-century ladies always had a dainty top half, thanks to the corset. But it wasn't without pain, and the 1840s corset was not a comfortable garment. It had a flat length of wood or steel up the center front and strips of whalebone up the back, and sometimes down the sides. The corset was pulled in and laced until the lady thought her waist was tiny enough (and felt she could still breathe, just about). It was stiff, uncomfortable, and the lady was in danger of fainting if it was done up too tightly.

Petticoat problems

Crinolines were enormous metal-hooped cages worn under skirts to make them stand out, and they were all the rage in the 19th century, when the fashion was for huge billowing skirts. This made getting through narrow doorways and into carriages tricky, and strong gusts of wind could bowl a lady over. Crinolines were partly made from fabrics like muslin and silk, so just one spark from an open fire could spell disaster for a lady and her crinoline.

A Method Of Recording Dance Movement

Benesh Movement Notation (BMN) is a way of recording ballet (and other dance) steps on paper. It was developed by Rudolf and Joan Benesh in 1955 and it is still used today. BMN uses symbols to represent the position of dancers' hands and feet as seen from the back. It is written on a "stave," which is a set of five horizontal lines, and each line shows the position of a different part of the dancer's body. Here are three very simple examples.

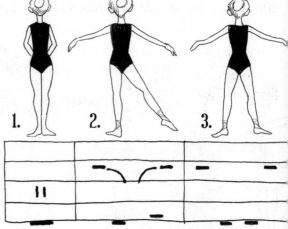

1. Both feet are level and together on the floor. Both hands are held in front, just below waist height.

2. Standing on the left foot, with the right foot pointed above floor height. The arms move up and outward, from waist height to just below shoulder height. The movement of the arms is indicated by the curved lines.

3. Both feet are level, standing apart at shoulder width. Both hands are level and held out at just below shoulder height.

Things You Don't Want To Join Your Ballet Class

An Ihuaivulu is a huge, mythical South American creature with seven heads. Ihuaivulu lives in a volcano and is prone to breathing fire, posing extreme danger to girls wearing synthetic tutus.

A Cyclops comes from Greek mythology. This hideous and violent giant has one eye in the middle of its forehead. Cyclops is noted for cannibalism (so there is a strong possibility he will eat you), rather than being graceful on the dance floor. He will not fit standard ballet shoes.

Charlie Chaplin, the famous silent-film star, once entered a "Charlie Chaplin lookalike" contest. He came third.

How To Knit With Your Fingers

Finger-knitting is a fun and simple way to knit without using needles. Follow the steps below to make a long strip of knitting. You could wear it as a stylish hairband. Once you become an expert, you could knit strips in lots of different colors to wear with different outfits, or to give as presents.

1. Choose a ball of wool. Wrap the end of the wool loosely around the index finger of your left hand (or right hand if you are left-handed) and tie a knot in it. The short end of the wool should be hanging down the back of your hand.

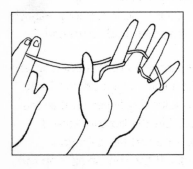

2. Weave the "working end" of the wool (the bit attached to the ball) behind your middle finger, in front of your ring finger and then behind your little finger. Make sure the loops are not too tight.

3. Now weave back to your index finger, so the wool goes in front of your little finger, behind the ring finger, and so on. Then repeat steps **2** and **3**, so you have two loops of wool on each finger. The second weave of wool should lie above the first weave.

4. Starting at your little finger, lift the bottom loop of wool over the top loop. Slip it off your finger and drop it behind your hand. Repeat with the bottom loop on your ring finger. Continue in this way until all four fingers have only one strand of wool wrapped around them.

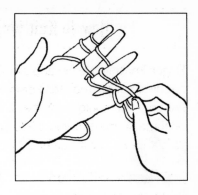

5. Start weaving again, so you have two strands around each finger. Then repeat step **4.** Every so often, gently pull the knitted strip behind your hand to keep it tight and in shape. Keep going until you have a knitted strip behind your hand that is long enough to go around your head.

6. To finish the hairband, make sure you are at a point where there is only one loop of wool on each finger. Lift the loop off your little finger. Slip it on to your ring finger, so that this finger holds two strands of wool. Lift the bottom strand on your ring finger over the top one and slip it off your finger. Drop it behind your hand. Lift the remaining loop off your ring finger and slip it on to your middle finger. Repeat until you are left with one strand on your index finger. Cut the wool off the ball, leaving a 15cm (6in) tail. Feed the tail through the remaining loop. Slip it off your finger and pull it tight to secure the end of your knitting. *Voilà!*

Eight Ways To Make A Hamster Happy

1. Buy the biggest cage you can afford. A plastic hamster home or wire cage with a plastic base is best, not a wooden one, as your hamster can chew its way out. Make it multi-level, and split into resting, feeding, and playing areas.

2. Position the cage carefully. A place where there is no direct sunlight or draughts, and an even temperature is best. Avoid putting it near anything with constant noise, like a fridge or freezer, or near a TV or CD player.

3. A hamster wheel must be big enough so your hamster doesn't have to bend its back inside, and solid, as rungs can hurt its feet and tail.

4. Hamsters love to play. A sisal rope is good for your pet to climb and gnaw on, and toilet-roll or kitchen-roll tubes are fun for it to run through. Small pots and plastic pipes make perfect hiding places. Remember to avoid anything wooden, as a hamster will chew its way through in no time. Switch the toys around sometimes, so your hamster doesn't get bored.

The happiest hamster in the world.

5. Make your hamster work for its food. Wild hamsters spend hours foraging for food, so keep your hamster busy and active by hiding its food in boxes and pots in the cage.

6. Clean the cage regularly. Each day, take out any soiled bedding. Each week, change all the bedding, sweep out the cage and rinse with warm water and detergent. When it's dry, put in clean bedding (not synthetic bedding, as it can block cheek pouches, and the digestive system). Give your hamster plenty of material to build a nest.

7. Check your hamster regularly. Look for wood shavings trapped in its coat and remove them with a special hamster brush or soft toothbrush. Check its coat is clean and shiny. Check its eyes, ears, nose, and under its tail for any sign of sore areas.

8. Remember that hamsters are "nocturnal" (active at night). They exercise three to four hours a night, but sleep a lot in the day. They don't like being woken suddenly any more than you do, so wake your hamster gently … and never pick up a sleeping hamster – it might bite you!

Reflex Test

A reflex is an automatic reaction your body makes to something. It happens so fast you don't even think about it.

Some examples of reflexes are:

- Coughing
- Sneezing
- Whipping your hand away when you touch something hot
- Sticking your arm out to catch a ball that is flying toward you
- Blinking when something flies towards your eye
- Knee-jerk.

Try this tapping test with a friend to test your knee-jerk reaction.

1. Sit on a chair with your knees bent.

2. Cross one leg over the other, with the upper foot hanging above the ground.

3. Get your friend to give you a quick sharp tap with the side of their hand just below your kneecap.

4. Your leg will jerk up in a kicking reaction.

The killer whale is the fastest swimming mammal. It can reach speeds of 55km/h (34.5m/h). The gentoo penguin is the fastest swimming bird at 35km/h (22m/h).

National Flowers

A national flower is a symbol that represents a country. The origin of a country's national flower is often linked to cultural or religious events in history.

Austria	edelweiss	Ireland	shamrock
Belgium	red poppy	Japan	cherry blossom
Brazil	orchid	Mexico	dahlia
Egypt	lotus	Netherlands	tulip
England	rose	Portugal	lavender
France	iris	Scotland	thistle
Germany	cornflower	Wales	daffodil.

Do You See A Musician Or A Girl's Face?

Music Terms

Many of the words that are used to describe music are Italian. This is because they were first used by important Italian composers.

Crescendo: Getting louder

Diminuendo: getting quieter

Piano: Quiet

Pianissimo: Very quiet

Forte: Loud

Fortissimo: Very loud

Accelerando: Getting faster

Adagio: Slow

Allegro: Quick and bright

Andante: Flowing, at a walking pace

Cantabile: In a singing style

Dolce: Soft and sweet

Espressivo: Expressively

Legato: Smooth

Presto: Very quick

Rallentando (rall.): Getting slower

Staccato: Detached

Vivace: Fast and lively.

If Only It Happened In Real Life

It would be great if some of the cool things that happen in books could happen in real life. Just imagine, you could have …

… a fairy godmother, like Cinderella.

… a cloak of invisibility, like Harry Potter.

… a wardrobe leading to another world, like in *The Chronicles of Narnia*.

… a chocolate factory, like Willy Wonka in *Charlie and the Chocolate Factory*.

… a faun as your best friend, like Lucy in *The Chronicles of Narnia*.

… Mary Poppins as your babysitter.

… a secret unicorn, like Lauren's pony, Twilight, in *My Secret Unicorn*.

… a magic finger, like in Roald Dahl's *The Magic Finger*.

Wonderful (Untranslatable) Words

The following words have wonderful meanings but they can't be directly translated from their original language into any other. Your friends and family will be left tongue-tied the next time you casually drop them into conversation.

Bakku-shan is a Japanese word. It is used to describe a girl who looks pretty from behind, but when she turns around she's not. Ouch!

Esprit d'escalier comes from a French phrase, which literally translates as "the spirit of the stairs." It describes that *really* annoying situation when you think of a brilliant comeback to something someone has said to you, but it's too late.

Jayus is Indonesian slang meaning a joke that is so terribly bad you can't help but laugh – try it the next time one of your friends thinks they are being hilarious.

Katahara itai is another Japanese term. Have you ever laughed so hard that your sides hurt? This is the feeling of "katahara itai," and a great feeling it is, too.

Leberwurst spielen is a German phrase that everyone is guilty of doing sometimes – it means to stick your lower lip out in a sulk (in German, the phrase literally means "to play the insulted liver sausage").

Tartle is a word from Scotland describing that moment you hesitate when you are introducing someone because you can't remember their name. Awkward!

Tingo is a great word. It comes from Easter Island, an island in the eastern Pacific Ocean. It means: "to borrow objects from a friend's house, one by one, until there's nothing left." Do you know anyone who might be guilty of a bit of "tingo"?

Uitwaaien is a Dutch word, meaning "walking in the wind for fun." And why wouldn't you?

....

Unlucky!

....

Some things that are believed to be bad luck in different places around the world:

- Walking under a ladder
- Breaking a mirror
- The number 13
- Friday the 13th
- Seeing a single magpie
- Keeping shoes upside down
- Leaving a hat on the bed
- An umbrella open indoors
- Whistling at sea
- Clipping nails at night
- Spilling salt
- Washing hair on a Thursday or Friday.

Fun Time-Travel Destinations

If you could travel back in time, it would be fun to drop in at …

… a Roman banquet

… the very first Olympic games in 776BC

… a society ball in 18th-century Europe.

Diva Demands

True divas always demand difficult things. Try these at home so you're ready when stardom strikes (and if you are successful in achieving them, you are well on your way to becoming a true diva).

"My bath should have a bath pillow and a drinks-holder, and please scatter rose petals on the water."

"Ensure all my meals contain at least four different colors of food – and no foods should be touching."

"Anyone leaving my presence must walk backward, bowing until they are told to stop."

"The sitting room is too dreary for a diva. Please redecorate with polka dots, all two centimeters in diameter."

Pop diva Lady Gaga wore a dress made entirely of meat to the 2010 MTV Video Music Awards.

Safari Animal Footprint Guide

White rhinoceros

Elephant

Hyena

Cheetah

Gazelle

Hippopotamus

Zebra

Lion

Giraffe

Baboon

Some Countries And Their Capital Cities

Argentina	Buenos Aires	Morocco	Rabat
Australia	Canberra	Netherlands	Amsterdam
Belgium	Brussels	New Zealand	Wellington
Canada	Ottawa	Pakistan	Islamabad
Chile	Santiago	Portugal	Lisbon
China	Beijing	Qatar	Doha
Croatia	Zagreb	Russia	Moscow
Denmark	Copenhagen	Spain	Madrid
Egypt	Cairo	Sweden	Stockholm
Ethiopia	Addis Ababa	Switzerland	Berne
France	Paris	Taiwan	Taipei
Germany	Berlin	Thailand	Bangkok
Ghana	Accra	Turkey	Ankara
Greece	Athens	Uganda	Kampala
Hungary	Budapest	UK	London
India	New Delhi	USA	Washington, DC
Italy	Rome	Vietnam	Hanoi
Japan	Tokyo	Yemen	Sana'a
Kenya	Nairobi	Zimbabwe	Harare.

How To Avoid Burping

- Don't talk with your mouth full.
- Don't use straws.
- Don't chew gum.
- Take your time eating.
- Don't have soda.

Earth Layers

Imagine drilling through the surface of the Earth, all the way to the center – these are the layers you would travel through.

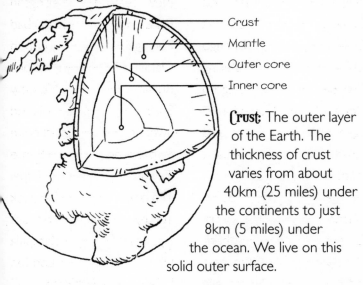

Crust
Mantle
Outer core
Inner core

Crust: The outer layer of the Earth. The thickness of crust varies from about 40km (25 miles) under the continents to just 8km (5 miles) under the ocean. We live on this solid outer surface.

Mantle: The thick layer of rock under the crust. It extends to a depth of around 2,900km (1,800 miles). With temperatures reaching nearly 2,000°C (3,600°F), the mantle rock is so hot that it has partly melted into thick, gooey molten rock called magma.

The core: The Earth's core is so deep below the surface, scientists aren't entirely sure what it is made of. The outer core is about 2,250km (1,400 miles) thick and is liquid. The inner core is the center and hottest part of the Earth – over a scorching 7,000°C (12,600°F)! It is thought to be solid due to the layers above pressing down on it.

Skipping Stones

Follow these steps to become a stylish stone-skipper. Find an area of calm water to practice your skills. Pick a stone that's round and flat and fits in the palm of your hand – slate works best.

1. Stand side-on to the water and bend your knees so you are nearer the water's surface.

2. Tuck your middle finger under the stone, and grip the edges with your thumb and index finger.

3. Keep your eye on where you plan to throw the stone.

4. Pull your hand back, then flick your wrist forward as you throw. Use your wrist and index finger to spin the stone as it leaves your hand.

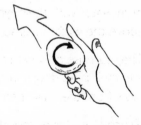

Top tip: Keep your throw flat and low, rather than angling it upwards.

Once you've perfected your skills, why not hold a competition with your friends? The first person to skim a stone that "bounces" six times on the water before going "plop" wins.

The Crocodilian Fact File

"Crocodilian" is the term given to a specific group of reptiles, made up of 14 types of crocodile, seven types of alligator and caiman, and one gharial (also called gavial). So what do you need to know about these cool creatures?

- Crocodilians were around in dinosaur times, but they were bigger than they are today, measuring up to 12m (39ft) long. That's as long as a bus!

- They like to snack on fish, frogs, wading birds, reptiles, mammals up to the size of water buffalo – and, of course, occasional humans.

- These reptiles like to loiter near riverbanks or waterholes, or in water with their eyes and nostrils just poking up above the water level so they can see what's going on.

- They surprise prey with a sudden leap out of the water, grab it in their jaws, drag it into the water, stun it with a heavy blow from their tail, then drown it. What a way to die!

- Crocodilians have smooth skin on their bellies – which used to be popular for handbags and shoes.

- They don't cry, but saltwater crocodiles shed tears to get rid of the salt in their eyes.

Dessert Named After An Opera Singer: Peach Melba

Peach Melba was created in honor of Australian opera-singer Dame Nellie Melba. Around 1892, she visited the Savoy Hotel on a trip to London, and a famous chef named Auguste Escoffier created a dish for her, based on her favorite summer fruits, peaches and raspberries.

For four people, you will need:

250g (2 cups) fresh raspberries • juice of 1 lemon • 4 scoops of vanilla ice cream • 1 tbsp icing sugar (powdered sugar) • 1 can peach slices • handful of flaked almonds (optional).

1. Mix together the raspberries, sugar, and lemon juice in a bowl.

2. Place a sieve over a small bowl. Gradually pour the raspberry mixture into the sieve and use the back of a spoon to push and crush the mixture through the sieve. Continue until all of the liquid is drained from the seeds and you are left with a raspberry sauce in the bowl.

3. Drain the peach slices and arrange them in bowls or glasses. Top with one scoop of ice cream per bowl.

4. Pour the raspberry sauce over the top and finish with a sprinkling of flaked almonds if you are using them.

WARNING: MAKE SURE YOU LEAVE OUT THE NUTS IF YOU OR YOUR FRIENDS OR FAMILY HAVE A NUT ALLERGY.

In the 1960s, straight hair was very fashionable but there were no flat irons, so some girls used an actual clothes iron. Do not try this on yourself!

Sense-Sational: Taste

You know if something tastes good (like gooey chocolate cake or yummy ice cream) and you definitely know if something tastes bad (like the vegetables you hate but have to eat because they're "good for you"). But what is taste?

Smell makes up almost three-quarters of your sense of taste, which is why everything tastes the same when you have a cold or your nose is blocked. A human tongue has between 2,000 and 8,000 taste buds but they are far too tiny to be seen. Your mouth makes a new set of taste buds every 10 days, and it is said that a good night's sleep makes your taste buds work better.

Bitter
Sour
Salty
Sweet

Different parts of your tongue detect different flavours. There are four basic flavours – sweet, sour, salty, and bitter – as well as a fifth savoury taste called "umami" which means "yummy" in Japanese. Spicy food gives your taste buds overload, and they can take 24 hours to work properly again.

The American painted lady butterfly has taste receptors on its feet. The butterfly walks on its food to taste it.

The End

Finished

Finito

We are like, so done here

I'm outta here

That's all folks

Thank you, thank you

This is the end.